Kids Like

Learn To Read
There's a Monster in the Tree
Learn To Read
Barney Bear, World Traveler
Learn To Read
The World in a Supermarket

We like to read.

We like to write.

We like to draw.

We like to paint.

We like to play.

We like to build.

We like lunch!